Discovering Moons

Judith Valente

Judith Valente

To Jane,
With appreciation
for all you do to bring
poetry into the lives
of others. May you find
in these poems something
to comfort, challenge
and delight.
Best always,
Judy

VIRTUAL ARTISTS COLLECTIVE
http://vacpoetry.org
ISBN: 978-0-9798825-8-6

Several of these poems originally appeared in the chapbook *Inventing An Alphabet*, selected by Mary Oliver for the 2004 Aldrich Poetry Prize, sponsored by the Aldrich Contemporary Art Museum, Ridgefield, CT.

"Green" was the recipient of a $1,000 Poetry Award from the Illinois Arts Council.

"Body & Soul" was selected by Paulette Roeske as the first place winner of the 2005 Jo-Anne Hirshfield Poetry Prize.

Grateful acknowledgment is extended to the editors of the publications where the following poems first appeared:

TriQuarterly: "Green," "Faces of the Madonna," "Winter Journal," "In Ka'anapali," "Central Illinois, Late October"

Rhino: "Why Write"

AfterHours: "Inventing An Alphabet" (titled "Alphabet"), "Letter to the Dead," "Wabi Sabi," "The Future of the World" (titled "Awaiting the Millennium"), "Morning Docket," "Dancing In Place," "Discovering Moons," and "Sunflower Field"

Free Lunch: "The Book of 55,000 Baby Names"

Folio: "Conjugating"

Twenty Poems To Nourish Your Soul: (Loyola Press, 2005): "Body & Soul"

Where We Live: Illinois Poets (Kathleen Kirk, editor. Great Unpublished, 2003): "Run for Your Life" and "Summer Parade, Old Route 66"

The Best Catholic Writing, 2004 (Brian Doyle, editor. Loyola Press, 2004): "Conjugating"

National Catholic Reporter: "The Call"

The Final Lilt of Songs: The South Mountain Poets Anthology: "After Dabney's Barbershop"

For my poetry mentors, Marie Howe,
Rosellen Brown, Susan Hahn, and
Joseph Parisi, and as always,

For Charley,
you're every line, every word

Table of Contents

Body & Soul

Walking With Dr. Williams

Why Write

Body & Soul

Green

You remove each article of clothing,
    discharge your fingers of each ring:
        Grandma Costanza's garnet birthstone,
14-carat fealty ring from Galway. One contact lens,
    then the other, gold cross on a chain.
        Dispossessed now of all identifying factors
except the unerasable: black mole
    on left calf; ovate beauty mark
        beneath right breast.

They want the body unadulterated:
    marrow, muscle, bone, cartilage
        – a dresser drawer emptied of all dust,
pennies, paper clips in the slats. They want the house
    tenantless, the deck scrubbed
        and white-washed, the diamond
driven back to carbon, the skin stripped to dermis,
    wrapped now in the flimsiest of polka-dot cotton,
        less than even the dead get.

You are grateful to the point of tears
    for the anesthesiologist whose name
        you can't remember. He brings a pea-green
blanket, warm as if from an oven, enthuses, *Great veins.*
    Offers a double aperitif of Versed, Sublimaze.
        Just a pinch, then a slight stinging feeling.
You cannot imagine why you didn't notice before:
    how every nurse looks like an unripe
        cornstalk, moss-colored mushroom
            blooming from each head.

When did you begin menstruating?
    Have you ever been pregnant?
      Had a sexually-transmitted disease?
Questions you've never answered even for your lover
    who is standing just outside
      behind a thin curtain. Questions
you discuss now with four strangers,
    two of whom wheel you through self-opening
      doors, lift you onto a white table,

extend your arms outward,
    tape them to a board, tie your feet,
      slip oxygen tubes into the keyholes of your nostrils
as the fluorescent lights above bloom into hydrangea,
    soften, fall, fade to black. They will excise
      the bodily intruder who arrived undetected,
squatted on your land, began to breed. A strip mining scar
    soon to be inspected, dissected:
      fistulous or fibrous, pigmented or pale,
        naughty or nice?

You drift back gently to a green world:
    grass-colored scrubs, aqua chairs, mint walls.
      You walk now as if your legs descend like bark
through linoleum, piping, concrete and I-beams
    deepening into the orange earth. At night,
      dream of a bald blue man who beckons
with a beautiful hand, invites you to the other side,
    but you won't go. You make the sign of the cross three times.
      He filters into air. You awaken, a penitent
        to the gray, marsupial morning.

———

In Ka' anapali

Hurtling through night at 497 miles per hour,
    the sea a black berth, clouds crumpled top sheets,
        I, who hate to fly. Window seat

near the starboard engine, each engine
    blasts out 37,000 pounds of thrust,
        rotates 12,000 times a minute,

so at night in bed in the dark mouth of Maui,
    motion still spools through me, a strange blood.
        We sleep a punctured sleep,

awaken to paradise:
    to the sound of a waterfall, the distant
        What now, what now of a rainbowed Macaw,

to banyan, litchi and bronze Manjuari,
    god of Wisdom, and eight bald-headed,
        pot-bellied Luhan disciples of Buddha

kneeling beside a hau tree: all, I imagined
    you storing up to show me,
        in a language in love with vowels:

Alaloa - long trail
    heiau - stone temple;
        kilo hoku - to observe the stars.

The sea too has a voice, but does it have
    a language? The sea as it was our first morning,
        a child playing tag with the shore,

a shore that is never "it." The signs
    on Ka'anapali warn of dangerous shore breaks,
        jelly fish, sea urchins, man of war.

This is where the silversword
    grows for fifty years,
        blooms a single day, then dies.

Late afternoon on the lanai, we watch
    the sky flame from mango
        to smoke to berry-blue, you say

a 100 million galaxies
    is proof of the existence of God. I choose
        memory, the night we lie side by side

on a hammock talking of everything
    and nothing: gibbous moon,
        unbroken sky, Venus dropping

and Mars ascending. Both of us
    conscious of the red stars, the dying,
        grateful for the white stars, still being born.

Body & Soul

When you enter the world, you come to live on the threshold
between the visible and invisible.
John O'Donohue, "Eternal Echoes"

Imagine those moments
 after the soul leaves the body.
  Imagine the body's immense
loneliness: a manse emptied
 of its single boarder. A child
  banging its fists against the living
room window, begging for its mother
 to *Come back!*
  as the car jerks out of the driveway
– for all the child knows, forever –
 and there's that awful last glimpse:
  back of a head growing smaller, smaller
through a rear windshield.
 This is why we should stay
  close to the body after death,
the way we used to hold wakes, at home
 and around the clock, until the body adjusts
  to its noiseless status, widowed rooms.

The monks of St. Lleuddad
 labored to pinpoint the seat of the soul.
  Day and night in a dank cellar
they sliced through blackening corpses,
 the abbot settling finally on the pineal gland:
  cross-section of cranial concavities,
disengaged from the grosser parts of blood.
 How does the soul disengage?
  Shoot like air from a depressurized cabin?
Drift through a cracked window

———

12

like the musk scent of a summer house?
Does it seep like runoff, spurt like blood
from a severed vein, or exit in stages,
an actor drinking in final bows?

John O'Donohue says we should
think of death not as the breath
on the back of the neck,
but a companion with us since birth,
benign doppelganger who knows us
better than we know ourselves
That's not to say
we're like Schrödinger's cat,
at once dead and alive –
but death we carry with us,
close as the fine hairs caressing
our skin. Of course, John is a theologian.
I prefer physics. Julian Barbour's concept:
time, a continuous tableau of many
different nows, each a single frame
passing an all-seeing lens,
so the instant of me in my kitchen
a few minutes from now,
stirring a can of Campbell's tomato soup
for lunch in 2001 Chicago,
rolls out in simulcast
with Andy Warhol applying a splotch
of fire-engine red to his soup labels
in 1962 New York.
We are at once fetus and 44 years old,
molting in the Big Bang
and reading this poem.

Where does the soul go?
    Meister Eckhart was asked.
        Nowhere, the great mystic replied.
He believed an invisible world
    lies just inside the visible,
        which would suit me just fine
because there is so much of this world
    I'd miss and want to hold on to,
        like Nick at the N&G Grocery,
saying *Artichokes, we have artichokes*
    before I even ask, and
        Next year we go together to Greece;
Earl Grey tea and cinnamon scones;
    this afternoon sun, waving a yellow hand
        across my neighbor's balcony,
falling like a spotlight on the roof
    of the Chicago Historical Society
        where the Stars & Stripes
dance a samba with the wind;
    this snow, spread like steamed milk
        on the sidewalk beneath my window;
this red terry cloth robe I'm wearing:
    spiral note pad, No. 2 pencil
        stuck inside its pocket.

Run For Your Life

    Is it true some people
can foresee their own death? Like John F. Kennedy
    peering into that open-roof limousine
from the top floor of a Hilton months before Oswald,
    saying *Somebody could really get you.*
Or Private William L. Lynn at 15, writing home
    from San Diego, *Oh Mom hurry. Soon as possible*
If you can, try to get me out by Sunday. Bring some clothes
    when you come, and three months later
in the Bataan peninsula, a bullet sails through his neck.

        Today, walking
to mail some packages, I spot a crowd
    gazing up at an office tower, and a man says
a window fell from the 29th floor
    of the CNA Insurance Building, sliced through
a woman's head while she was walking with her daughter.
    That's what came out of her. He points
to a puddle of something brown, red and gray
    lying in front of the PMI Parking lot:
blood, skin and brain tissue like rain-soaked Kleenex.
    The blood dark like car oil, already drying.

        Picture that woman
who took the bus or train downtown. One minute
    she's walking along Wabash Avenue,
holding her little girl's hand. The next, she's barreling
    through the after-life. *As unpredictable a death*
as exists, a friend of mine says later. This strikes me
    because just last week I was reading W. S. Merwin's
"For the Anniversary of My Death" where he says
    every year without knowing it, we pass

———

the date of our death. Now passersby gesture
    toward the CNA building as if to say,

            That's the one, there's the perpetrator,
half expecting the police – who have whisked away
    the child and thrown up yellow cordons –
to slap handcuffs around the CNA, its pink frame
    always calling attention to itself. Now every building
beats with the heart of a potential murderer,
    though the Beaux Arts cut a *bella figura,*
look less suspect than the Art Deco ones.
    Only the wrought-iron facade of Carson Pirie Scott
inspires trust: an English gentleman
    with gapped teeth in black tie, tails.

            I imagine
that woman's name, though no one knows it yet,
    how perhaps she went to Mass on Sundays,
cooked with cumin and cilantro, felt bored
    by the smell of her own bed sheets. How she
probably has a husband at work somewhere
    at a Boudin's bakery or Chevy dealership,
(though tomorrow the papers will say she was
    Anna Flores, 36, of South Spaulding Avenue,
downtown to pick up a job application). And I hope
    her little girl is young enough for the mind
to toss a black veil over this afternoon,

            like John F. Kennedy Jr.
saying he remembered nothing of his father's funeral
    though it took place the day he turned three.
I think of the ways I've worried death could
    catch me, like walking into a gunfight
some Friday at the Mid-City National Bank,

———

or an aneurysm: exploding firecracker in the brain.
Hoping death wouldn't just show up at my door,
    a discourteous guest, but drop a note in the mail,
say months, years in advance,

            as polite company would do,
so I'd have time to imitate Ben Gazzara
    in *Run For Your Life,* travel to a new city
each week helping complete strangers
    find their passion in life. Time to tear up my journals,
press the clothes in the laundry basket,
    finish the crosswords on my nightstand,
toss out my torn underpants and apologize for decades
    of bad behavior before removing the robe of life,
    folding it neatly, not letting it fall.

Faces of the Madonna

Mary tightens her lips in Botticelli's
"Annunciation," pushes back the angel

as if to say: *Do your work. You will
never possess me.* Fra Angelico's virgin

sits amid arches and cypresses, blonde
and wafer-thin, shawled in blue velvet.

The butterfly hands cross her chest.
Their creamed porcelain suggests

the marble stairs of Pilate's palace.
These are not the hands of my mother,

a bottle blonde, olive skin so dark
that when she tanned, her sisters called her

netta in Sicilian: negress. My mother
who would not wash my hair for weeks

for fear I'd catch a cold, washed my father's
scalp and feet because she thought

he should not do these things for himself,
slipped away Wednesdays to St. Michael's Church,

the afternoon Novena, placed a dollar bill
in the plastic bin beside a blue Madonna:

———

ice goddess with downcast eyes, out-stretched hands,
prayed my brother would be spared Vietnam.

To you we cry, poor banished children of Eve.
To you we send up our sighs, mourning
and weeping in this valley of tears.

Praying the words over and over, and my brother
didn't go, though his orders were written

his name was on the list. Tessie's miracle
they called it. I at five, silent in my pew

did not yet see this world as a field of pain,
held my mother's hand like a rope

thrown to a drowning child as we walked
home past the shops on Broadway,

she in her open-toe shoes, her lamb's wool coat
brushing my side, like the 13th century

"Mother of Mercy" (Umbrian artist, name unknown)
who opens her cloak, envelops the world:

monarch, soldier, peasant, bishop.
La Madonna della Strada. Hail, holy queen.

———

Conjugating

I was the only public
that September at St. Aloysius

third desk from last
the alphabet outskirts of class

only Jane Zaccaro,
Barbara Zombrowski

farther asea
My body a stranger

in alien clothes
pleated skirt, white knee socks

Peter Pan collar
buttoned to the neck

In freshman art
Mrs. Cirone asked us

to observe a beechwood
describe what we saw

and some said summer
others said nature

I said the branches
were the serpent tresses

of Medusa – we had read
Bulfinch's Mythology

in Sister Helen Jean's
Latin class –

the bark the terrible
wide stem of her neck

Mary Smith grimaced
Doris Crawford then

Maureen Jennings snickered
their laughter spread

washed over the waste baskets
George Washington's portrait

the crucifix above
the blackboard in Room 202

I wanted to run from that place
in my stiff new regulation loafers

from the girls who lived
in stone houses on Bentley

and Fairmont Avenues
summered at Avon-by-the-Sea

knew by heart the Apostles Creed
the Joyful, Sorrowful

and Glorious Mysteries
but I knew my mother

at that moment stood ankle-
deep in red rubber boots

in a pool of gray water
hosing down cucumbers

at Wachsberg's Pickle Works
so she could earn $1.05 an hour

squirrel away a few dollars
each week to pay my $600 tuition

and at three o'clock
when Sam Wachsberg blew

his plastic whistle, remove the boots
pack up her lunch sack

take home the Broadway bus
smelling of sweet relish

pickled onions
while the school kids sniffed

her clothes, laughed
behind her back

I learned to calculate the square root
of a hundred twenty seven

memorized the Holy Sonnets
the symbols of the elements

mastered each declension
and conjugation:

amo, amas, amat

Central Illinois, Late October

The season spills out its fistful of playing marbles:
     millefiores, sunbursts, oxbloods, caneswirls.

Bronzed leaves hang:
     gnarled hands emptied of pennies. Death smell hangs,
      moist fomenting cider in the tight-chested ground.

I steady myself for the cardboard colors to come:
     Dun, amber, sepia seeping over ungrazed prairie.

Saturday. The afternoon drive past
     Dwight   Odell   Pontiac   Towanda

Familiar markers rise
     like white crosses for the roadside dead:
      Sun Motel Pete's Harvest Table Robert Bolen Stock Farms

Whether castle
     hut or geodesic dome
         Guns save lives
            in our homes

take root beside cross-stitches of corn, soybean
     soon to dissolve, absolve in a font of 5 p.m. cobalt blue.

Spring is an *O* of astonishment.
This, this is the pursed lip of a *B,* mouth slammed shut
on the tongue. Steel casing snapped
     in place over a coffin: gunshot blast in the woods.

Weather report:
>*What are conditions outside?* She asks.
>*What are conditions inside?* He answers.

We dangle between eternity
>and the dry, uncertain landscape,
>>*tabula rasa* and our own wavering perspective
>>>as tonight in the gallery, we study the vertical rods
>>>>of a Julia Mangold sculpture:

He hears music. B natural, C sharp.
>She sees four flat waxed steel girders, dirty-brown.

Lunar Eclipse

Amber, occluded eye
more iris now than pupil
whose dark-lashed lid

droops slowly downward,
succumbs to night's hypnosis.
Earth falls from memory,

a bead lost in cobalt light.
The Buddha, it is said,
had a thousand eyes

to watch the world
with compassion. Tonight,
a million pairs of eyes

fix on the one dreaming eye
suspended beyond
earth's sorrowful drumbeat,

the humming of the sun.
Saturn to the west.
Regulus to the east:

a universe at peace.
Sun, moon, planet
aligned, like patches

of a quilt, as if peace
were a cloth we could
cuff in our hands,

rub between our fingers,
and the only language
that matters, silence.

The Call

Not the long, sad moan
    of a train whistle

or fist of wind pounding
    the bedroom window.

Not the paw tap across
    a linoleum floor,

or shriek in the night
    from the dark street.

Not the hum in the back
    of the throat, the buzz

inside the ear. Not the drum roll
    of rain or thunderclap,

but the quiet before thunder:
    a warm breeze ambling

through a closed room,
    ruffling a flowered curtain.

Then the soul spirals downward,
    enters the unfused crown.

It is the falling in dreams,
    a falling with seemingly no end.

The grass stirs.
    A doe lifts her head, listens.

The Book of 55,000 Baby Names

Some, like the Inoa, look for long-gone
ancestors to send a message in a dream or vision.

Hopis place a husk of corn next to an infant's ear
and wait for inspiration. Tutsis pair

names to conditions at hand. Abena means *arrived
on a Thursday.* Iniko: *born in troubled times.*

My step-daughter Rachel, awaiting her first, plumbs pages
of "The Book of 55,000 Baby Names." This tome gauges

how Emily and Emma reached the top of the roster,
waving their white pom-poms like long-legged cheerleaders,

how John fell out of fashion with platform shoes
and madras jackets, displaced by Aidan, Ian and Sean,

how Michael and Matthew, like bargains and beer, never go
out of vogue, along with Mary, Jesus, Jose and Joe.

Rachel (named for no one in particular)
settles on Ava, Portuguese for grandmother,

Number 31 this year. Classic, but not common,
with its hint of the first woman.

Some still enter this world nameless,
like the newborn preemie, dark-haired, restless,

lying in the crib next to Ava's in the neo-natal ward:
no crayon-colored name on his white ID card.

He punches the air with a balled fist, then lifts
his swaddled bottom. Name him, *Adia,* Swahili for gift.

Driving In Snow, Thinking of Ava, One Month Old

Snow tumbled
    peaceably all morning
        from a cadmium sky,

wrapped the spindly evergreens,
    the black locusts' bare arms
        in a thin white yarn.

It was the white of Elijah's robe,
    the pure white of gesso,
        the newborn's white sight

before the world takes on
    its geometric forms. The white of sleep,
        of thought and the moon

on a mid-December night,
    as if God had white-washed
        commotion, that cranky old man,

and his temperamental cousin,
    despair, then picked up
        a whetstone and chisel

to begin again: a block of Tuscan marble,
    the white noise of waking,
        an infant's sweet and sour scent.

Walking With Dr. Williams

Home

Three-posted shelter for me, *O me*

The *om* I release to center myself:
Breathe in, breathe out

The instinct that drives
us back to where we started:
XX marks the spot

Where the heart (hearth) is or isn't

Casa, [caza], chez moi
heim, I'm, as in

I'm these bookshelves
suede couch   brass table
bowl of oranges

The object we seek:
Home plate. Home base.
Home office. Homestead

Domov. Domicile. *Dominus.*

The domestic gods we harbor:

Grandma's Wedgwood china
carved creche from Bethlehem
first edition *Leaves of Grass*

Where the homely is handsome

The grave (long home)
we come to reside in

What we leave (leap) in the end:

Deruta bowl
Two-carat diamond earrings
Waterford pen

How many homers?

11 1/2 bushels, 100 gallons:
this heap.

Kome Loy

Three pairs of hands rise disembodied against a blank November sky in the black and white photograph my stepdaughter Meghan has snapped.

It is the night of the northern Festival of Lanterns. Chiang Mai. First full moon of the twelfth lunar month.

She has steadied her grip, slowed the shutter speed to an eighth of a second to capture the instant the hands thrust rice paper lanterns into hot air flight.

Hands raised in prayer. I say. *Creepy apocalyptic,* she says. *Like some cult worship thing.*

The torches release the sins and pain of the past year: the broken bones, benders, infidelities, wagers gone bad, here in the land of the 'lucky' this, the 'paradise' that.

Even the dead prawns tossed on ice in Chiang Mai's outdoor market are prized for their "happy eyes."

My stepdaughter teaches art to teenagers at the Prem Tinsulananda International School. She has fashioned a dark room from scraps: two porcelain basins, a clothes line, some tin food trays.

I wish I could remove the worm of pain from her heart as deftly as the fingers, shining like filaments, float these paper ghosts on a sea of chilly moonlit air.

———

Tonight in the doll house temple, I will leave an offering of jackfruit, plate of sticky rice, thimbleful of whiskey. I have heard the gods drink whiskey.

Return from the Desert

Each thorn was like a dagger the doctors removed from his
                                        chest with pliers:
A boy believes he can take a machete to a saguaro without
                                        consequences.

A stranger crushes the leaves of the creosote, says, *Smell the
                                        scent of desert after rain.*
A scent of sun, dust and water. But what is the antecedent,
                                        what is the consequent?

The Papago Indians say their god, *I'ito,* lives on the highest
                                        peak of the Baboquiviri Mountains.
The Kikuyu say God makes a home on Mount Kenya.
                                        Collective memory is not inconsequential.

Jesus cursed the fig tree because it would not bear fruit. But
                                        from an altar of burning fig branches,
the Kikuyu saw African fathers rise from the ashes. Myth flows
                                        from such odd sequences.

From an altitude of 40,000 feet, the western landscape cracks
                                        and rolls like leathery skin.
Who lives in a town called Truth or Consequences?

We soar past the checkerboard fields, circular irrigation wells of
                                        Kansas. Of so much
green and gold, bread is the consequence.

At Picture Rocks, the stone feet of the Virgin crush the head of
                                        serpent. Rain pours down Mary's
face like tears. I tell myself it is of no consequence.

Forty at my birth, my mother named me Judy after the patron
                              saint of hopeless causes. I longed to
be biblical Judith, savior of a desert people, a woman of
                                        consequence.

To The Man Who Says He Doesn't Dream At Night

He closes his eyes, drifts off
    on an inflatable raft of theta brain waves.

The pons taps out a Morse code
    to the thalamus, cerebral cortex.

Neurons surge through circuitry
    dense enough to under-gird

the city of Washington. They arc, flame,
    and go blank.

He does not ride the back fender
    of a taxicab across a sea of urine,

or rise up on a geyser to grab an airplane wing
    mid-air with his bare hand,

or suffer the panic of the door that will not lock
    to the dark house, where lizards

drip off the tips of a spider plant.
    He does not walk barefoot in slush,

forgetting the spot he's parked the car,
    or sip chamomile with dead aunts

at the flowered ironing board table.
    He wakes to sunlight

———

seeping through beechwood branches,
    notes in Cyrillic script

on the blank page of his bedroom wall:
    white handwriting of morning.

After "Dabney's Barbershop"

To love you, I must love
    the way Matisse
loved the egg: so much

he sketched one every morning
    for years on end,
the charcoal pencil tensed

in his hand to trace
    the curve just right,
his eye lost in a dozen shades of white.

I must love also
    this rust-dripped
elevated track, the dragon drone

of the silver train as it floats past
    on its steel throne,
leaving a taste of rust and slate.

And I must love the hand warmth
    of the coffee cup,
veins of parched ivy skulking up

its yellow sides. Love equally
    the quasars heating up
our distant galaxies:

they roll through space
    like a child's slinky,
sing their billion-year- old melodies.

And I must love
   the teetering barbershop
stuck in the middle of the block

in the sad white painting.
   The shop slants on its side
like a version of the truth,

blonde filaments of youth
   powder the barber's checkered floor,
like your dark, homuncular

shavings, mornings
   in the white basin. To love
you, I must love a world of venial

sins and Sunday quiet, a blue
   room with white borders,
a claw-foot tub, and you inside it.

Summer Parade, Old Route 66

When I turn off the interstate,
swerve down the exit ramp,

beside a still-green corn field,
you are waiting. You stand alongside

a Cutlass convertible, gold
with champagne bank seats.

I slip into the passenger side,
we crest toward town without seatbelts,

me curled into your side. "Last Kiss"
on the AM oldies station:

Where oh where can my baby be?
The wind runs its bony fingers

through our graying hair,
enters us completely. We compete

to remember the characters' names
on "Route 66." *Buzz, yes! ... and Todd,*

tell each other not in words
our lives are just beginning.

At the Wishing Well, Mitzi
our waitress, serves up buckwheat cakes,

a sausage patty the size of Sausalito,
a Dixie cup of orangeade.

We meet Bud, the Republican Party
chairman, and Earl, a sheriff's candidate

who won the primary by just 23 votes,
and now carts a bucketful of peppermints

he'll hand out to the kids who've lined
Waiponsie and West for this Sunday fest

of politicians, John Deere harvesters,
fire trucks, classic T-Birds.

I ask if we can stop inside "the old
Catholic Church." (Nobody in Odell

calls it St. Paul's). You wait outside
– say it's been a long time – then

slide into a pew, kneel beside me.
This too is love. This too is love-making.

One day I may push you away. You may
wound me. The utility of heartbreak.

We watch the sulfur butterflies,
yellow and white, blink on and off

in the jagged grass beneath us. We listen for
their wing beats, our syncopated breath.

———

Morning Docket

Weather-worn farm houses,
aluminum grain bins, and listing pinwheel

wind towers interrupt
the level landscape: beneath desiccated corn stalks

a fresh powdering of snow.
We coast along Route 117 through a soft focus

lens of early morning mist,
bound for Eureka. The courthouse rises

like a khakied sentinel in the town square.
You don your black Solomon's robe.

A young man refuses to pay
a thousand dollar fine, receives thirty days

for his DUI, asks for time to say goodbye
to his small daughter, his wife, thin railing

of a girl, possibly nineteen,
with stringy, auburn hair. The deputy breaks

their thin embrace, leads the man away
in handcuffs. The young wife

slaps her child across the face
because the little girl will not put on her coat.

Through the swinging doors
the child's shrieks haunt the deserted corridors.

But you are listening now to a woman
who rolls before you in wheelchair,

wants a restraining order against
her husband who threw the family's

cocker spaniel across the Christmas dinner
table at their sixteen-year-old pregnant daughter:

*"For seventeen years, I've lived
in a torture chamber with this man."*

Last year at this time I was burying
a mother, you a thirty-year marriage.

In Dwight, police still search for a man
they suspect smothered his two children,

bundled them into his Chevy Caprice,
then tossed their bodies off the bridge

over the Des Plaines at Channahon,
still wrapped in a Snoopy blanket.

Someone planted a white cross,
painted the names: Joshua 4 Ashley 3.

At 5:15, we will drive home past
Busy Corners, the Barn Dinner Theater,

Marge's Flower Basket under a third-
quarter moon, holding each other's hand.

Our neighbor's daughter
will run to greet us with the day's riddle:

Why did the crab turn red?
Because he saw the salad dressing.

We will set a table of eggplant,
bread, black olives, an Australian Shiraz.

In bed, you will read me
the letters in The Pantagraph,

your body burnished in lamp light.
I will turn to you and say,

How did we become so blessed?
You will answer, *Don't ever ask.*

Jesemy-By-The-Sea

Daylight chalks a thin white line across the horizon,
We wake to the mockingbirds' *cur-cur*.

Later: the white-throated thrum of a cicada's castanets.
Soon we will go to the sea,

build a house of flotsam for our desire.
If we toss our shelled memories from shore,

the sea returns them with a low moan rising,
still whole, but changed now like the white sand

we shake from our sun-burnt feet entering the house
called Jesemy. The day runs on without commas, dashes.

We speak the language of silence.
White the sun, white the sea beneath it.

White the sheets. White my breasts beneath
your tanned hands. White the mind of the moon we wait for.

How else could I have told you of the mystery:
white seeds stashed in the palm prints of morning?

Reading Rumi on Hatteras Island

This is love: to fly toward a secret sky.
Jelaluddin Rumi

Love should be heart-less.
For the heart, that jagged amethyst,
conceals within itself the bitter pit of our desire.

Having washed the feet of shore,
love rests in the arms of sea,
to begin again its solemn enterprise.

Once man and woman were whole.
Knowledge of good and evil
tore them asunder.

Once land and sea were one,
now they age in shared longing.
The shore catches what secrets the sea offers,

returns them as the dunes give back
sand to wind. Love sits upright on the shore,
longs for the stranger, sudden light of recognition,
as night hungers for moon.

Walking With Dr. Williams

He bids a dry farewell
  to the crying babies,
    impetigo, scabies

ringworm, croup and hives,
  the spider bites
    gone haywire.

He bundles the Number 4 sutures
  into antiseptic drawers,
    locks the tetracycline,

penicillin behind glass doors,
  stows the steel needles
    in their steamy autoclave

while upstairs Flossie prepares
  the butcher block table:
    salmon cakes, baby peas, pommes dauphine.

At dusk we roam
  the banks of the Passaic
    where a cojo fisherman

calls out some lines
  from Longfellow:
    Like a huge organ, rise the burnished arms . . .

He bows and smiling passes,
  says how like a kumquat
    the fisherman's bell

---

dangling from a grocery cart.
　　He instructs me to shout
　　　　the names of what we see

and I do:
　　gaggle of geese, dusty miller, cumulo-nimbus . . .
　　　　We dissect the day's words:

Viburnum, saxifrage, intra-cutaneous,
　　our tongues larded
　　　　with dactyls, trochees.

Late at night in the damp attic
　　at a desk where Flossie has placed
　　　　almond cookies, Twinings with real cream

he will clip the Dow Jones Index,
　　tape it to a wall
　　　　wrap a blanket around his shoulders, write

　　　　The instant

trivial as it is

　　　　　is all we have

　　　　　　unless, unless

Why Write

Winter Journal

The willow sees the heron's image upside down.
Basho.

These days even the stars seem poisoned.

I wake with a cream donut lodged in my brain.

At church they gave thanks for Monsignor Smyth, cured of leukemia.

Then he died.

Mornings I tell Michael I can't go on like this.

And he says, here, eat these flowers I have picked.

I feel words fold their fingers around my shoulders.

Frangipani tongues on my neck.

Now I think: these walls are not so pink.

12 million anonymous people. 4,500 beats an hour.

144,000 forms of torture.

It was as if we navigated by a Dickensian map.

Inanition. Verbing. Words as salvation.

I came to writing through a fear of forgetting.

There once was a man who killed himself after his lover died.

They say he could not bear to hear the word Spring.

Inventing An Alphabet

Can it be all writing began with a stick man, his left foot
      frozen in a can-can kick, waving his arms overhead

as if shouting *Whoopee?* The father of our letter H,
      the scientists say who discovered him not long ago

carved into a limestone cliff west of the Nile,
      across from the royal city of Thebes,

where he had danced undisturbed for 4,000 years
      beside the ox head that elongated into an A,

the upside down spoon that sprouted into a B,
      giving birth to Alpha and Beta,

alpha males and beta males. The one: men who
      fool around on their wives, the other: men

who would like to fool around on their wives; and Rimbaud's A –
      a black belt hairy with flies; Emily Dickinson's 1,775 poems,

Dante's nine circles, *Do ron ron ron ronda do ron ron* and
      Whan that the Knyght had thus his tale ytoold,

Ask not what your country can do for you,
      See the USA in a Chevrolet, *What you want, baby I got it,*

M-I-C-K-E-Y M-O-U-S-E and Good night, Sweet Prince.
      Odes and onomatopoeia, haiku and heroic couplets,

---

elegies, acrostics and acronyms like Ph.D., PMS, U.N.
    and U.N.C.L.E (as in The Man From),

all because some Semitic tribesmen tired of the grim dust
    of Palestine, advanced to another forlorn desert,

a place in southern Egypt called Wadi el-Hoi,
    "Gulch of Terror,"

concocted a simpler way than pictographs.
    This: the earliest known alphabet.

Each semi-cursive symbol flowered into a single sound,
    one sound slid into the other to harvest a word.

Stealing thunder from the elite hands of the Egyptian scribes,
    they passed their new-found, hard-won shorthand

to Canaanites, Phoenicians, Greeks and eventually you and me,
    and isn't laziness so often the mother of invention?

(Consider White Out, Minute Rice, Post-Its, garage door openers).
    Then it became an easy Scrabble board leap from yellow to ecru

honey to sunflower, buttercup, lemon and goldenrod.
    To Spanglish and Esperanto and the 10,000 ways we have

of saying hateful things, like *tu madre*, *va fa n'culo* and *je m'en fout.*
    Whether one reads the alphabet left to right,

right to left or up and down, it's only a matter of time
    before *Mein Kampf*, Machiavelli, the Marquis de Sade

———

and Denise Richards growing letter by letter in a thong bikini
      on the Internet. And who can even imagine

the first words cooked up in this new alphabet soup?
      Maybe *Mama, water, help*

or simply, *me*. Perhaps nothing as unabashed
      as "I love you," which I once saw

spray-painted on a railroad overpass,
      addressed to a girl named Joannie, encoded as 1-4-3.

Discovering Moons

What happens, happens in silence.
We wake in a room your daughter painted

sunrise red. Daylight drips through linen
curtains, feeds us intravenously.

Like Galileo with his scope
unearthing Jupiter's moons, we lie on our backs on the white

clay of our bed, chart the constellations of ceiling.
That Y-pronged crack you call a ballerina *en pointe*

in fifth, her arms flung above her
about to slide into an arabesque,

I say is Christ strung upon his cross
moments after earth shuddered, temple curtain tore apart.

On a shelf in the living room,
a brown box contains all that remains of your mother:

every pigment of bone, muscle, cilla, cartilage.
One day you will spread such fine matter

across the mining hills of Edwardsville,
the coast of Ventura, the prairie outside of Normal.

In soundless desert, astronomers discover
new moons: 45 in the last six months around Jupiter alone.

There is so much I want to say to you
in a language without words. We orbit each other

like the moons circling Jupiter
in unconjugated space: Europa, Callisto, Leda, Ganymede, Thebe.

(The first line of this poem is from "Private Lives" by Lisel Mueller.)

The Future of the World

A supernova might erupt
with an assassin's rage,
and the earth crumple over, a corpse,

the coffin snapped shut on
every living proton, which would mean
the end of Lyon & Healy harps,

every C-string ever to play
a note of Debussy,
every cathedral and concertina,

all of Shakespeare's 154 sonnets,
Baskin and Robbins' 31 flavors.

A gamma ray buster could
roast us chickens on a spit,
rain radiation like herb butter,
then flame out without a trace.

Beware of hypernovas,
those black holes that stalk
the sky in pairs like grizzlies,
their bellies full of neutrons. They belch
and, *voila,* a celestial bomb blast.

Keep an eye on the particle accelerator
at the Fermi Lab in Batavia.
All day long protons collide
at two trillion electrovolts a pop –

it could punch a hole in the stratosphere,
plunge every cow and cow pie in Batavia
– not to mention the rest of us –
into that *awful all-becoming nothing.*

Perhaps a giant vacuum lies behind
the heavens, a great Dust Buster
poised to one day suck us up
like so many flies on a sill,

or, perhaps like our own human hearts,
the universe is running down
and will one day stop,
the way a wind-up toy flops.

This could be trillions of years away –
maybe 10 to the 33rd power in years –
when my DNA, and yours,
is little more than lava ash,

or, it could be just around the corner,
which is why I eat Dipsey Doodles
for breakfast, leave the crumbs on the table
and the crossword puzzle half done,

and when I walk it is to feel the planet
beneath my feet: grass, mud, gravel, concrete,
the weary earth, here and today.

Wabi Sabi

Osgood Schlatter's
is hobbling you again:
snakes strangling your knees.
And when you walk

you list
from that old inflamed
Achilles heel, high school
football injury

At night,
dry lips, stiff fingers, occasional
bloodshot eye. *The chassis
is breaking down,* you say

and I say
Wabi sabi, a term I learned
from our handyman Dale
as he fingered the nicks

in Mother's
china cabinet: the art of finding
beauty in flaws. Tonight
I will run my fingers

through your graying
chest hair, kiss the arrow-
shaped bald spot on your crown,
moisten your chafed skin

with my tongue,
ride the slopes of your jagged
breathing, whisper *wabi sabi*,
my rhombus-shaped

diamond of
inclusions. You are not
the pomace, but the cider,
not the kindling but the shoot

Memorial Sloan-Kettering

David's mother wheels him across the deck
    outside of pediatrics
        St. Patrick's Day morning.
            He wants to feel the sun on his neck

Purple crocuses
    in red flower boxes lift their tongues to the sun
        a chill wind crosses the parapet.
            David sends his mother back inside for a blanke

Jesus will pull him through
    David's mother tells the Moslem chaplain.
        She doesn't care what God the chaplain prays to:
            Allah, Jehovah, Bahá'u'lláh

For 20 years the imam has washed and shrouded
    bodies at Malcolm Shabazz,
        swears he's seen smiles
            on the faces of the dead

David draws his blanket
    across white slipper socks, striped flannel robe.
        Dilaudid flows from his broviac line
            in a thin rivulet

Who will inscribe him in the book of life?

After Rain

for John Mug

After five days of rain
the vermilion geraniums
in the window box
spend their last coins
on the dying season.
Their slender stems,
blossom heads, bow now
like mourners at a funeral.

At a hospital in St. Louis
a friend of my husband's
awaits a new pair of lungs
(Lung, from the German
lungen for lightness)
to replace the aluminum
cylinder of breath he drags
at his side like a third arm.
(Breath: akin to steam, vapor;
in some contexts, spirit).

The morning folds into
a prayer of thanksgiving,
Sibilance of rain
sounds out the whispered
words of a rosary:

Our Father,
who art in heaven,
hallowed be this body,
its shroud of flesh,
its dark chambers,

hidden cargo, its delicate
and mysterious industries.

Dancing in Place

Jimmy Roberts died a few months ago,
    my mother tells me
the day after Thanksgiving. We sit side by side
    watching a rerun of The Lawrence Welk Show.
Lawrence's orchestra in full bravado –
    matching mustard-colored blazers –
as tasteless as it got in the '70s unless you consider
    burnt orange, magenta and avocado.

Jimmy is the tenor with the pompadour
    who sang "All The Way"
and "I Give To You and You Give to Me"
    with fluty Norma Zimmer,
who unlike Jimmy is still alive, but *God,*
    she's aged, my mother says,
a statement I find odd
    since my mother always looked much older

than Norma even after she became
    a honey blonde from the bottle.
To introduce the rerun they've brought back
    Myron Floren, the accordion player,
now a shaky-voiced senior
    newly recovered from heart disease,
kidney stones and colon cancer.
    He thanks Welk fans for their prayers,

then Myron (who frankly still looks pasty
    to me) says the hardest part
was not being able to play the accordion
    for eight months. He straps on
the gleaming black-and-white chest,

launches into "Lady of Spain"
for all you ladies out there...
            And though I detested

these people: Myron, Norma and Jo Ann Castle
            of the prancing piano fingers,
Joe Feeney the Irish tenor,
            and *the lovely Lennon Sisters,*
who, let's face it, even with ring curls
            and capped-teeth weren't so lovely,
for invading our living room Saturday nights,

back in the days when my teenage head rang
            with lyrics of Joni, Elton, Carly and James,
my eyes well up now at the sight of Lawrence
            and my mother, stooped as Grandpa
when he was her age, eighty-five. She jiggles
            her swollen feet to "Hernando's Hideaway"
on a blue reclining chair, flashes

the yellowed toenails the podiatrist
            will trim next week
as the Amaryl courses through her over-sugared
            blood doing, or not doing, its work.
Cissy rhumbas with Bobby. She wears a Carmen Miranda
            get-up. He's in Ricky Ricardo sleeves.
My father perks up on the La-Z-Boy
            when the orchestra breaks into the theme

            from "The Prime of Miss Jean
Brodie," a movie I'm certain he's never seen
            and surely wouldn't approve of,
crooning *Come into the meadow bonnie Jean,*
            seeming much younger than eighty-nine,

------

tapping his dusty loafers in time
    as we all three are fading, dissolving to blank,
like the pinpoint in the center of an old
    Philco black and white.

Sunflower Field

for Yolanda Ericson

*If you want to know what I believe about
the after-life,* she said, *read this book.*
She had moved on from Elisabeth-Kubler Ross,

discovered the British spiritualist W.S. Stead
who perished on the Titanic, and slicing
the veil between this life and the next,

channeled messages from the other side through
his daughter's hand (though experts vouched
it was *his* writing), described a 'Blue Island'

of domed houses, neatly parceled fields
filled with every species of bird and flower,
where you were still yourself, only more so:

same tang of anger, fistful of resentments
and all the old appetites. Where you spent your days
(for there were days) working to forget each sin,

the past's dim faces, shedding a little each time
of the old self, like dead skin. Once after
she tumbled back to this life from the other,

she told us she had listened to music. We asked
was it Mozart or Miles Davis? She said it was
celestial music like no scale she'd ever heard.

And on those days when the cancer
rampaged through her body like a hungry dog
and her eyes turned into dark, stationary clouds,

she kept reaching up for something,
something out of sight. The ledger she called it.
I've got to write my name in the ledger.

We asked then if she saw the fields.
She nodded. We said tell us what they're like.
Sunflowers, she said. *Endless, open sunflowers.*

Letter to the Dead

The leaves lingered longer this autumn,
outwitted the forecasters
who expected their peak

the third week of October.
A shower of meteors swung across the sky
in mid-November,

precision tumblers of combustible light
we won't see the likes of until 2090,

and scientists mapped the portion of the brain
where violent tendencies simmer to boiling,

announced a packet of 300 genes separates us
from our cousins, the field mice.

Perhaps you know all this already,
wherever you are,
which is for certain where I am not.

I still eat artichokes, take Italian lessons
on Wednesdays, have fallen behind in the ironing

and who knows just how close to Christmas
I'll push it before the cards go out this year.

Odd the things that remind me of you:
the way daylight dribbles in through the drapes
just so,

———

throws a single spindle of amber light
        on the bedroom wall;

that brown leaf bleeding into the sidewalk
        in early December,
awaiting snow's erasure;

        or the iridescent Kelly-green star I spot
stuck to the stone floor of a rest stop
        in Marion, Illinois.

Perhaps this is the *real* real world C.S. Lewis spoke of.

        The man I love flies back from Abuja,
tells me grains of sand whipped up
        in a Saharan storm

can travel as far as a parking lot in Key West.
        So much of what exists

        we never see:
think of magnetic waves, photons,
        isotopes, quarks.

        Day after day, we tend
to the new among you:
        bathe bodies, moisten them with oil:

sandalwood, jasmine, rosewater;
        wrap them in linens – three for males,

five for females – turn them toward the East.
We massage the crowns,
dress in black, keep watch with the *chevra kadisha,*

tear our clothes, wash our hands,
cut our hair, leave pebbles, plant flowers,
etch names into stone:

"*Theresa, Beloved Mother.*"
"*Timothy, Loving Husband.*"

and try to subsist on our "feast of losses."
Yit-gadal v'yit-kadash sh'mey raba:
Hear, O Israel, the Lord our God is one.

The astronomer says
there is a place in the universe where stars form
before they begin their long death march

toward earth's atmosphere:
a place of pure light.

Eternal rest grant unto them, O Lord,
and let perpetual light shine upon them

I name you
Mother, Mike, Kerry, Lupe, Lorraine, Miguel, T.J., Terry, Paul

the dead that I have known,
suspend you like stars in that space

where light doesn't die,
doesn't even dim.

Why Write

I want to give you
something of comfort:

words like an armoire
smelling of talc, lined

with lace, concealing
a ruby bracelet, tortoise

shell comb. Words
that melt on the tongue

a communion wafer,
wheaten and whispering of salvation.

Words the color of Beaujolais,
glazed garnets filled

with fire, fire and blood,
words the scent of wood smoke

on a black marble autumn night,
that swing open their arms,

(the Corcovado Christ,
ever welcoming, forgiving)

a Braille of my heart,
to finger as a rosary bead,

to bloom a vermilion crocus,
this Spring and many Springs.

Judith Valente is an on air correspondent for PBS-TV and Chicago Public Radio and contributing correspondent for National Public Radio. She worked previously as a staff writer for *The Wall Street Journal*, *The Washington Post* and *People* magazine. She is the author of the poetry chapbook *Inventing An Alphabet*, selected by Mary Oliver for the 2004 Aldrich Poetry Prize. She is co-editor with her husband, Charles Reynard, of *Twenty Poems to Nourish Your Soul* (Loyola Press, 2005), an anthology of poems and reflections on finding the sacred in the everyday, winner of a 2008 Eric Hoffer Book Award citation. She is the recipient of an Illinois Arts Council Poetry Award and the Jo-Anne Hirshfield Poetry Prize. Her poems have appeared in *TriQuarterly*, *Comstock Review*, *Ninth Letter*, *Free Lunch*, *Rhino*, *AfterHours*, *Illinois Poets: Where We Live*, and *Best Catholic Writing of 2004*. She has given workshops across the country exploring the connection between poetry and photography and poetry and spirituality. She is currently at work on a non-fiction book about contemporary monastic life.